WHERE WE GOING, DADDY?
DADDY? WHERE WE GOING,

Life with Two Sons Unlike Any Others

JEAN-LOUIS FOURNIER

translated by ADRIANA HUNTER

with an introduction by FERN KUPFER

OTHER PRESS
New York

Cet ouvrage a bénéficié du soutien des Programmes d'aide à la publication de Culturesfrance/Ministère français des affaires étrangères et européennes.

This work, published as part of a program of aid for publication, received support from CulturesFrance and the French Ministry of Foreign Affairs.

Production Editor: Yvonne E. Cárdenas
Text Designer: Simon M. Sullivan
This book was set in 10.5pt Berthold Baskerville by
Alpha Design & Composition of Pittsfield, NH.

10 9 8 7 6 5 4 3 2 1

LIBRARY OF CONGRESS CATALOGING-IN-PUBLICATION DATA
Fournier, Jean-Louis.
[Où on va, papa? English]
Where we going, Daddy? : life with two sons
unlike any others / by Jean-Louis Fournier ; translated by
Adriana Hunter.
p. cm.
ISBN 978-1-59051-338-5 (pbk. original with flaps)–
ISBN 978-1-59051-384-2 (e-book)   1. Fournier, Jean-Louis.
2. Authors, French–20th century–Biography. 3. Authors,
French–21st century–Biography.   4. Parents of children with
disabilities–France–Biography.   5. Fathers and sons–France–
Biography.   I. Title.

PQ2666.O853895Z46 2010
848'.9203–dc22   [B]   2009041139

INTRODUCTION *by Fern Kupfer*

Our second child, Zachariah, a much wanted son, looked perfect at birth. Most caesarean section babies do. As an infant, he had big blue eyes with long fringy lashes and downy blond hair that later grew into golden curls. But in the months following his birth, I noticed that he never held up his head; he didn't quiet when we came into the room and spoke in comforting tones. The tests to determine what was wrong began when he was around six months old and continued until he was more than three years of age. My son's first few years had passed without his reaching any normal developmental milestones: Zachariah did not hold a spoon, sit up, or say "mama." I didn't know it then, but he never would.

In Iowa, where we live, we get tornados. Once, when Zach was still at home, there were warning sirens for everyone to take cover. It was early evening when the tornado alarm sounded; Zachy was fast asleep, but the wailing sirens woke Gabi, our six year old. My husband found a flashlight, and the three of us stood at the top of the stairs for a moment as I looked at Zach's closed bedroom door. He was difficult to get to sleep and fretful all the time he was awake unless he was rocked and soothed or taken somewhere in the car. Often I drove him around in the car at five in the morning until it was only me who was crying. "You're going to take Zach down to the basement with us, aren't you?" Gabi asked, her eyes wide. Of course, of course.

It's natural for parents to love their children, but when you have a severely damaged child whose needs suck up all emotional reserve, whose future will never hold the pleasures of the most ordinary imagination, then love is the least of it. Truth be told, parents of damaged children sometime fantasize about the loss of our child in an instant, painless scenario. We can imagine a tornado tearing off the roof of a house and swooping a sleeping child into a peaceful land of Oz.

Parents of severely handicapped children do have dark thoughts. Most of the time we do not say them aloud, especially in a society that works to accept differences and sometimes canonizes the parents of "special" children as unselfish, strong, courageous. Americans in particular can be sentimental: our handicapped children are "angels"—sweet and innocent. They're needy, yes, but so very worth our sacrifices. Well-meaning people occasionally sent me the poem, "God's Very Special Child," whose couplets convey the message that we parents were even "chosen" by God:

And soon they'll know the privilege given
In caring for their gift from Heaven.

Although Americans are sentimental, we are also a practical lot who possess that "can-do" spirit, even toward the most limited of our population. Why else the push to "normalization," real jobs and independent living? Why else the cheering success of the Special Olympics?

Sentiment and practicality are not the primary themes of the book you are about to read. The author, Jean-Louis Fournier, is the father of not one, but two, severely handicapped children. Two, we are told on the very first page of *Where We Going, Daddy?* How can your heart not sink into your shoes? Fournier begins with a letter to his sons, Mathieu and Thomas, a letter in the form of a book that his boys will never be able to read. We see the boys always through Fournier's eyes. His sons disappoint. They make him feel guilty. As they grow older, they are not lovely to look at. The book is an apology of sorts to his sons for their very existence, for Fournier's own genetic contribution, which resulted only in "getting you so wrong."

Where we going, Daddy? is the question asked over and over and over again. Fournier gets exactly right the mind-numbing boredom of doing the same things and eliciting the same responses from a child who—except for his shoe size—does not grow. He captures perfectly the irritation, envy, and yes even rage that parents of handicapped children sometimes feel toward parents of the "normals"—parents who are ignorant of and oblivious to their own mundane good fortune; parents who share immodestly their children's accomplishments; or even well-meaning friends who, feeling sympathy, ask misty-eyed, "How are your boys?"

Fournier, who is also a comedic writer, channels his primal pain through humor. He uses his humor as a weapon, a defense against the pity of strangers or his own frustration. How is a father of not one, but two handicapped children supposed to comport himself? Fournier acknowledges that it takes "good manners just to look gloomy." He accepts that making fun of his own children and their severe limitations "is my privilege as their father."

I remember the private jokes as our privilege, too. "Close your mouth, you look retarded," Zach's father used to say, putting a few fingers gently under our son's chin to stop his tongue thrusts. If we don't laugh, we cry. Sometimes, we laugh and cry in the very same moment.

There was a play in the late 1960s that had a run on Broadway and was met with great critical success. The play was called *A Day in the Death of Joe Egg* and featured a married couple whose life was consumed by the care of their brain-damaged daughter, whom they referred to as "Joe Egg." The actress who played the daughter sat onstage in a wheelchair throughout, making spastic movements. Her dialogue consisted of unintelligible grunts and howls.

Perhaps because their daughter's personality was so unformed, her parents made up a capable and complicated persona for her. They might say, "Joe Egg wants to go for a walk in the park" or "Joe Egg thinks you're being awfully rash." They were not just speaking for someone who had no language; they were imagining their daughter into a healthy child with normal needs and desires.

A friend of mine saw this play in New York and told me that the audience response was generally shock followed by scattered, nervous laughter. Many were appalled. Except, that is, for those parents who knew, who said: *oh, yes, that's the way it is.* These are the unspoken, universal experiences that Fournier understands so deeply. On a drive, he asks of his boys in the back seat: "How's the trigonometry going?" What is a father to do but imagine, pretend, and make jokes?

Where We Going, Daddy?, which won the 2008 Prix Femina, France's prestigious literary prize, is not the usual tale of inspiration or tell-all confessional. The third child Fournier and his wife (optimistically or recklessly—depending on how you look at it) decided to go ahead with having was born normal and healthy. That daughter, Marie, is absent from the story. Fournier's marriage dissolves (as did mine to Zachariah's father), but we do not learn about his married life, and almost nothing is written about the boys' mother. All of that is, as Fournier says, "another story." This is not Fournier's autobiography. It's a pastiche of emotions, memories, and anecdotes that combine to form a deep and affecting picture of this particular kind of parent/child relationship.

There is some controversy—there always is, writing about one's life and interpreting or omitting the lives of others—following the book's publication in France. Would my ex-husband's account of our life together with Zachariah differ from my own? Yes, I am sure it would. In my writing classes at a university, I tell my students, this is your tale to tell. Leave out what you will. This is your life, your story. Everyone's version of family life may be different, but you must interpret the narrative to your own truth. Fournier's story is not every parent's story, but it is true and authentic, focused solely on the world he alone has shared with Thomas and Mathieu. This brief book is expressed in such a spare and uncluttered way that it reads almost like a prose poem. It is not a traditional narrative, but rather a series of impressionistic images, beautifully wrought.

> When I think of Mattieu and Thomas, I see them as
> two tousled little birds. Not eagles or peacocks, but
> modest birds, sparrows.
>   Their spindly little legs sticking out from under their
> short navy blue coats. I also remember, from bath time,
> their mauve transparent skin, like baby birds before
> they grow feathers . . .

The incredible pain and loss is universal for all of us parents, across both the gender and the cultural divide: the desire for what-could-have-been: games we will never play, books we will never share, loves we will never see bloom.

There is something that comes to all parents who have children like Mathieu and Thomas and my Zachariah. Even the most tough-minded truth-teller has had this longing: the fantasy of our children as whole, perfect. I still have dreams of walking into a room and seeing Zachariah there, smiling and pleased with himself. He looks up brightly as if to say, *Where have you been?* Often he speaks aloud in the sweetest, softest voice. The voice I imagined he would have if ever he could speak.

Like Matheiu and Thomas, Zachariah lived in a residential facility, looked after by a wonderful and loving staff of nurses and care-workers. His father and I visited, but eventually Zach was too fragile to be able to come for visits at home. After Zach died, I received letters from people who tried to comfort me by saying that Zach was now an angel in a place where he was set free. In my head I don't believe that, but in my heart—a mother's heart—I can see Zachariah as a young man, blond and blue-eyed and so handsome that all the girls turn to look as he runs by.

Without the brain-damage, the genetic misfortune, the missing enzyme, or added chromosome—who would our children be? Even Fournier, the least sentimental of writers, ponders meeting his sons in an afterlife:

Will we recognize each other? . . . I won't dare ask if you're still handicapped . . . Do handicaps even exist in heaven? Maybe you'll be like everyone else?

Will we be able to speak man to man, and tell each other things that really matter, things I couldn't say to you on earth because you didn't understand French and I couldn't speak Impish?

Perhaps in heaven we'll finally be able to understand each other . . .

Who's to say?

There are moments when this is not a comfortable book to read; it is not a story of how love and dedication can triumph over extreme adversity. There is no happy ending. But Fournier is honest in revealing the feelings of those of us whose children are irrevocably damaged. He gives permission and voice to these deepest, darkest, and most complicated emotions. And I believe that ultimately, it is only honesty that heals.

Where We Going, Daddy? bespeaks a fierce and lamenting love. Fournier dares to reveal the searing truth about a grief that has no end. And that, indeed, is a truth that must be told.

· · ·

FERN KUPFER is the author of the memoir *Before and After Zachariah: A Family Story About a Different Kind of Courage.*

WHERE WE GOING, DADDY?

Dear Mathieu,
Dear Thomas,

When you were little I was sometimes tempted, come Christmas, to give you a book, maybe one of the *Tintin* books. We could have talked about it together afterward. I know Tintin really well, I've read all of them several times.

I never did it, there wasn't any point, you couldn't read. You'll never be able to read. Right to the end your Christmas presents will always be building bricks and toy cars . . .

Now that Mathieu has gone chasing after his ball somewhere we can never help him find it, now that Thomas, who's still with us, has his head more and more in the clouds, I *am* going to give you a book. A book I've written for you.

So that you're not forgotten, and you're not just a picture on a disability card. So I can write some of the things I never said, perhaps some regrets. I haven't been a very good father; often I just couldn't take you, you were difficult to love. The two of you needed the patience of an angel, and I'm no angel.

To tell you I'm sorry we couldn't be happy together, and perhaps also to apologize for getting you so wrong.

We just didn't get lucky, you and us. It all landed in our laps, it's what they call bad luck.

I'm going to stop complaining.

When people mention handicapped children they put on a solemn expression as if they were talking about some catastrophe. For once I want to try and talk about you with a smile. You've made me laugh, and not always involuntarily.

Thanks to you, I've had various advantages over the parents of normal children. I haven't had to worry about your schoolwork, nor your choice of career. We never had to waver between the arts and the sciences. Didn't have to fret about what you would do later, we knew very early on what it would be: nothing.

And, more importantly, for many years I enjoyed the benefits of paying no road tax.[1] Thanks to you, I could drive a big American car.

---

1. Parents of handicapped children with a permanent disability card used to be exempt from paying any road tax. When the exemption was rescinded in 1991 there was no longer any advantage to having handicapped children.

From the moment he got into the Camaro, Thomas, aged ten, has kept on asking the same question he always does: "Where we going, Daddy?"

At first I answer, "We're going home."

A minute later, still just as genuine, he asks the question again—it's not registering. By the tenth "Where we going, Daddy?" I've stopped answering . . .

I'm not really sure where we're going anymore, my poor boy.

We're going with the flow. We're heading straight for a brick wall.

One handicapped child, then two. Why not three . . .

I wasn't expecting this.

Where we going, Daddy?

Let's take the freeway, against the traffic.

We're going to Alaska. We're going to stroke the bears. We'll be eaten alive.

We're going mushroom-picking. We're going to pick death caps and make a lovely omelet.

We're going to the swimming pool, we'll dive off the highest board . . . into the pool that's been drained.

We're going to the seaside. We're going to Mont-Saint-Michel. We'll go for a walk on the quicksand. And get sucked down. And go to hell.

3

Unperturbed, Thomas keeps it up: "Where we going, Daddy?" Maybe he'll improve on his record. By the hundredth time it really is a joke. You're never bored with him; Thomas is master of the running gag.

Anyone who's never worried about having an abnormal child, please raise their hand.

No one raises their hand.

Everyone thinks about it, just like we think about earthquakes, and the end of the world, the sort of thing that only happens once.

I had two ends of the world.

When you look at a newborn baby, you're full of admiration. It's so well put together. You look at its hands, count the tiny fingers, note that there are five on each hand, same with the toes: it's mind-blowing—not four, not six, no, just five. It's a miracle every time. Not to mention the insides, which are even more complicated.

Having a child means running a risk . . . You don't win every time. But people still keep on having them.

Every second on this earth a woman brings a child into the world . . . She really must be found and told to stop, added the comedian.

I remember the day we went to the convent in Abbeville to introduce Mathieu to Aunt Madeleine, who is a Carmelite nun.

We were taken to the visiting room, a small, whitewashed space. In the far wall was an opening closed off by a thick curtain. It wasn't a red curtain like they have in a puppet theater, but a black one. We heard a voice from behind the curtain saying, "Hello, children."

It was Aunt Madeleine. She's in a closed order so she's not allowed to see us. We talked to her for a while, then she wanted to see Mathieu. She asked us to put the stroller in the opening, and turn to face the wall. Nuns in closed orders are allowed to see young children, not older ones. Then she called the other nuns to come and admire her great-nephew. We heard rustling robes, chuckling and laughter, then the sound of the curtain being drawn back. Next came a concert of superlatives and ticklings and teasings for the heavenly babe. "He's so adorable! Look, Mother Superior, he's smiling at us, just like a little angel, a little Christ child . . . !" They came very close to saying how advanced he was for his age.

To a nun, children are first and foremost the Good Lord's creations, and are therefore perfect. Everything God makes is perfect. They don't want to see the failings. And, anyway, this was Mother Superior's great-nephew. For a moment I felt like turning around and telling them to stop laying it on so thick.

I didn't, though. I did the right thing.

To think Mathieu was being complimented for once . . .

I'll never forget the first doctor who had the courage to tell us that Mathieu was definitely abnormal. His name was Professor Fontaine, it was in Lille. He told us we should be under no illusions. Mathieu was backward, he would always be backward, either way, there was nothing we could do about it, he was handicapped, physically and mentally.

We didn't sleep terribly well that night. I remember having nightmares.

Until then the prognoses had been vague. Mathieu was a slow developer, we had been told it was only physical, there were no mental problems.

Lots of friends and relatives tried, sometimes clumsily, to reassure us. Every time they saw him they said how amazed they were by the progress he had made. I remember one time telling them that, as far as I was concerned, I was amazed by the progress he hadn't made. I was looking at other people's children.

Mathieu was limp. He couldn't hold his head up, as if his neck were made of rubber. While other people's children sat up arrogantly to demand food, Mathieu just lay there. He was never hungry, it took the patience of an angel to feed him, and he often threw up all over the angel.

If a child being born is a miracle, then a handicapped child is an inverted miracle.

Poor Mathieu couldn't see very clearly, he had fragile bones and in-turned feet, he soon became hunchbacked, he had thick shaggy hair, he wasn't beautiful and, more than anything else, he was sad. It was hard to make him laugh, he kept repeating a monotonous lament of "Oh dear, Mathieu . . . oh dear, oh dear, Mathieu . . ." Sometimes he was convulsed with heartbreaking tears, as if he couldn't bear not being able to tell us anything. We always felt he was aware of his situation. He must have thought, "If only I'd known, I wouldn't have come."

We would have loved to protect him from this fate bearing down on him. The worst of it was there was nothing we could do. We couldn't even console him, or tell him we loved him just the way he was: they'd told us he was deaf.

To think that I'm the author of his days, of the dreadful days he spent here on earth, that I'm the one who brought him here, I want to ask his forgiveness.

How do you recognize an abnormal child?

> He looks out of focus, distorted.
> As if you were seeing him through frosted glass.
> There isn't any frosted glass.
> He'll never be right.

Life isn't much fun for an abnormal child. It all goes wrong right from the start.

The first time he opens his eyes he sees two faces leaning over his crib looking at him, absolutely stunned. His mother and father. They're thinking, "Did we make that?" . . . and they don't look too proud.

Sometimes they yell at each other and foist the blame on each other. They trawl back through the family tree to find a great-grandfather or an alcoholic old uncle perching in its branches.

In some cases they split up.

Mathieu often makes "brmm, brmm" noises. He thinks he's a car. The worst thing is when he does the whole twenty-four hours of Le Mans. Driving right through the night without any pit stops.

I've tried several times to tell him to cut the engine, without success. It's impossible to reason with him.

I can't get to sleep. I have to get up early tomorrow. Sometimes terrible ideas come into my head; I feel like throwing him out the window, but we're on the ground floor, there wouldn't be any point, we'd still hear him.

I take comfort from the fact that normal children stop their parents sleeping too.

Serves them right.

Mathieu can't sit up. He has poor muscle tone, he's as limp as a rag doll. How's he going to develop? What will he be like when he's bigger? Will he need a stake like a sapling?

I used to think he could be a mechanic. But the lying down sort. The ones who work on the undersides of cars in garages where they don't have a hydraulic ramp.

Mathieu doesn't have many distractions. He doesn't watch television, he doesn't need its help to be mentally handicapped. There's only one thing that seems to make him slightly happy, and that's music. When he hears music he beats his ball like a drum, in time.

His ball plays a very important part in his life. He spends all his time throwing it in places he knows he can't get it back on his own. Then he comes to find us and takes us by the hand to the place he's thrown it. We get the ball back and give it to him. Five minutes later he's back looking for us, he's thrown the ball again. He's quite capable of repeating the performance dozens of times a day.

It's probably the only way he's found to make a connection with us, to get us to hold his hand.

Now Mathieu's gone to look for his ball all by himself. He's thrown it too far. In a place where we can't help him get it back . . .

It was nearly summer. The trees were full of blossom. My wife was expecting a second baby, life was beautiful. He was due to be born just as the apricots ripened. We waited impatiently, and a little anxiously.

My wife must have been worried. To avoid upsetting me, she didn't dare say so. But I did. I just couldn't keep my fears to myself, I had to share them. I couldn't help myself. I remember telling her with my usual tact, "Imagine if this one's abnormal too." I wasn't just trying to make conversation, more reassuring myself and warding off bad luck.

I definitely thought it couldn't happen a second time. I know those who love us most are best equipped to hurt us, but I don't think God loves me that much; I'm not *that* self-centered.

With Mathieu, it must have been an accident, and accidents don't happen twice; as a general rule, they're not repeated.

They say terrible things happen to people who least expect them, who never think of them. So, to make sure it didn't happen, we thought about it . . .

When Thomas is born he's gorgeous, blond with dark, dark eyes, an alert expression, always smiling. I'll never forget how happy I was.

He's beautifully crafted, a precious fragile thing. With his blond hair, he looks like a little Botticelli angel. I can't stop taking him in my arms, tickling him, playing with him, making him laugh.

I remember confiding to my friends that I could now see what it felt like having a normal child.

I've been too hasty with my optimism. Thomas is sickly, he's often ill, he's had to be hospitalized several times.

One day our family doctor has the courage to tell us the truth. Thomas is handicapped too, like his brother.

Thomas was born two years after Mathieu.

Everything's falling in line, Thomas will get more and more like his brother. It's my second end of the world.

Fate has been heavy-handed with me.

Even the corniest tearjerker TV film trying to make its hero heartbreaking wouldn't dare put something like that in the script, for fear of overdoing it, not being taken seriously and, ultimately, making people laugh.

Providence gave me the title role of the model father.

Do I look the part?

Will I be a good model?

Will I make people cry . . . or laugh?

"Where we going, Daddy?"

"We're going to Lourdes."

Thomas starts laughing, as if he understands.

With the help of a charity-worker, my grandmother has been trying to persuade me to go to Lourdes with my two boys. She wants to pay for the trip. She's hoping for a miracle.

It's a long way to Lourdes, twelve hours on the train with two kids you can't reason with.

They'll be better behaved on the way back, Granny said. She didn't dare say "after the miracle."

Anyway, there won't be any miracle. If, as I've heard say, handicapped children are a punishment from heaven, I can't really see the Blessed Virgin getting involved by performing a miracle. Surely she won't want to intervene on a decision made by a higher authority.

And when we get there, with the crowds, the processions, the darkness, I could lose them and never find them again.

Could that be the miracle, then?

When you have handicapped children you have to cope—on top of everything else—with quite a lot of inanities from other people.

There are those who think you deserve it. Someone who meant well told me the story of the young seminarian: he was about to be ordained as a priest when he met a girl and fell hopelessly in love with her. He left the seminary and got married. They had a child, and he was handicapped. It served them right.

There are those who say that having a handicapped child isn't a chance occurrence. "It's your father's fault . . ."

Last night I dreamed I met my father in a bistro, and introduced him to my children. He never met them, he died before they were born.

"Hey, Dad, look."

"Who are they?"

"They're your grandchildren, what do you think?"

"Not great."

"It's your fault."

"What are you talking about?"

"It's the absinthe. You know what they say, if the parents drink . . ."

He turned his back on me and ordered another absinthe.

There are those who say, "I would have smothered him at birth, like a cat." They don't have any imagination. You can tell they've never smothered a cat.

First of all, when a child is born, unless he has a physical deformity, you can't necessarily tell if he's handicapped. When my children were babies they were very like other babies. They couldn't feed themselves, like them; couldn't speak, like them; couldn't walk, like them; they sometimes smiled, especially Thomas. Mathieu smiled less . . .

When you have a handicapped child, you don't find out straightaway. It's like a surprise.

There are also those who say, "A handicapped child is a gift from God." And they don't mean it as a joke. It's rarely people who have handicapped children themselves.

When you're given this gift you feel like telling God, "Oh! you shouldn't have . . ."

When Thomas was born he was given a beautiful gift: a silver set of a tumbler, a bowl, and a baby's spoon. There are little embossed scallop shells on the spoon handle and around the rim of the bowl. He was given them by his godfather, the chief executive of a bank, who was one of our closest friends.

When Thomas grew, and his handicap very soon became obvious, he never had another present from his godfather.

If he'd been normal, I'm sure he would have gone on to have a lovely pen with a golden nib, then a tennis racket, a camera . . . But, because he didn't fit in, he was no longer entitled to anything. You can't really blame his godfather, it's a normal reaction. He must have thought, "Mother nature hasn't given him much, there's no reason why I should." The child wouldn't have known what to do with them, anyway.

I've still got that bowl, I use it as an ashtray. Thomas and Mathieu don't smoke, though; they wouldn't know how to, they're on drugs instead.

We give them tranquilizers to keep them quiet.

The father of a handicapped child is supposed to look gloomy. He has to bear his cross with a mask of pain. No way can he wear a red nose to get a laugh. He's lost the right to laugh, that would be the height of bad taste. If he has two handicapped children, the whole problem is multiplied by two; he has to look twice as unhappy, it's just good manners.

My manners have often let me down. I remember one time asking for an appointment with the head consultant at the special school Mathieu and Thomas attended. I confided my concerns to him: I sometimes wondered whether Thomas and Mathieu were completely normal . . .

He didn't think it was funny.

He was right, it wasn't funny. He didn't realize it was the only way I could think of to keep my head above water.

Like Cyrano de Bergerac who decided to make fun of his own nose, I make fun of my own children. It's my privilege as their father.

As the father of two handicapped children I was invited to take part in a television program to give a firsthand account.

I talked about my children, underlining the fact that they often made me laugh with the stupid things they did, and saying we shouldn't deprive handicapped children of the luxury of making us laugh.

When a child splatters his chocolate pudding all over his face, everyone laughs; if it's a handicapped child no one laughs. He'll never make anyone laugh, he'll never see laughing faces looking at him, apart from a few assholes laughing *at* him.

I watched the program, which was pre-recorded.

They'd cut out anything to do with laughter.

The producers felt they had to take parents' feelings into account. They might be shocked.

Thomas is trying to get dressed by himself. He's already put on his shirt, but doesn't know how to button it. He's now putting on his sweater. There's a hole in his sweater and he's chosen the difficult route: he's come up with the idea of putting it on, not by pushing his head through the collar, but through the hole. It's not easy, the hole can only be five centimeters across. It takes a long time. He can see we're watching and starting to laugh. With every attempt, he makes the hole a little bigger, but he doesn't give up, he goes at it with more determination the more he sees us laugh. After a good ten minutes he succeeds. His beaming face emerges from the sweater, through the hole.

The sketch was over. We felt like clapping.

It was nearly Christmas and I was in a toy shop. One of the salesmen was determined to help me even though I hadn't asked.

"How old are the children you're buying for?"

I unwisely gave an honest answer. Mathieu was eleven and Thomas nine.

For Mathieu the salesman suggested scientific games. I remember a boxed set for building your own radio receiver, it included a soldering iron and masses of electrical wires. And for Thomas a jigsaw puzzle of a map of France, with all the regions and names of cities cut out so you had to put them in the right place. I briefly pictured a radio assembled by Mathieu and a map of France put together by Thomas, with Strasbourg on the shores of the Mediterranean, Brest in the Auvergne, and Marseilles in the Ardennes.

He also suggested The Young Chemist set with which you could do experiments at home, making fires and explosions in all sorts of colors. How about The Young Kamikaze with his belt of explosives to sort the problem out once and for all . . .

I listened to the salesman's recommendations very patiently, thanked him, and then made up my mind. As I did every year, I took a box of building blocks for Mathieu and some toy cars for Thomas. The salesman didn't understand, he gift wrapped both presents without a word, then watched me leave with my two parcels. As I went out I saw him making a gesture for the benefit of his colleague, he was pointing his finger at his temple as if to say, "He's cuckoo . . ."

Thomas and Mathieu have never believed in Santa Claus, or in the baby Jesus. And why should they. They've never written to Santa to ask for anything, and they're in a good position to know that the baby Jesus doesn't give anyone any presents. Or, if he did, not ones you could trust.

We haven't had to lie to them. We haven't had to sneak off to buy their building blocks and toy cars, we haven't had to pretend.

We've never had a crèche or a Christmas tree.

There haven't been any candles, for fear of fires.

Or children's faces filled with wonder.

Christmas is just another day. The heavenly babe hasn't yet been born.

Some efforts are now made to integrate handicapped people into the job market. Companies who hire them are entitled to tax relief and lower charges. What a great initiative. I know a small country restaurant where two young men with slight learning difficulties are employed as waiters, and they're rather touching, they serve you so utterly willingly, but you have to be careful and avoid dishes with sauces . . . or make sure you're wearing oilskins.

I can't help picturing Mathieu and Thomas on the job market.

Mathieu, who often goes "brmm, brmm," could be a long-distance truck driver, hurtling across Europe at the wheel of a tractor-trailer weighing several tons, its windshield cluttered with teddy bears.

Thomas, who likes playing with toy planes and tidying them away in boxes, could be an air-traffic controller, he'd be responsible for bringing jumbos in to land.

Aren't you ashamed, Jean-Louis, you of all people, their own father, making fun of two little kids who can't even defend themselves?

No. It doesn't mean I don't have any feelings.

For a time we had a live-in nanny to look after the children. Her name was Josée, she was from the north, a blonde with a ruddy complexion, a sturdy girl who looked like a farmer's wife. She had worked for a number of distinguished families on the outskirts of Lille. She asked us to buy a bell to call for her. I remember her wanting to know where we kept the silver. In her previous job she used to clean the silver once a week. My wife told her we kept it in our house in the country, but one day Josée came there and, of course, there was no silver . . .

She was perfect with the children, full of common sense. She treated them like normal children, not too weak or excessively affectionate, she knew how to be tough with them when she had to. I think she really loved them. When they did something silly I often heard her say, "Oh, your heads are full of straw!"

That's the only accurate diagnosis anyone's ever made. She was right, Josée was right, they must have had heads full of straw. The doctors didn't even spot that.

Our family photo album is flat as a fillet of sole. We don't have many pictures of them, we don't feel like showing them off. Normal children are photographed from every angle, in every pose, on every occasion; you see them blowing out their first candle, taking their first steps, having their first bath. People look at them and go "ah." They follow their progress step by step. With a handicapped child, no one really feels like following their fall.

When I look at the few pictures we have of Mathieu, I have to admit he's not beautiful, you could tell he was abnormal. We, his parents, couldn't see it at the time. To us he even seemed beautiful, he was the first. Anyway, everyone always says "a beautiful baby." Babies have no right to be ugly, or at least, no one has any right to say so.

I have one picture of Thomas that I really like. He must be about three. I've positioned him inside a huge fireplace, sitting in a little armchair among the ashes, between the andirons, where you would light the fire. Where you would expect to see the devil, there's a fragile cherub, smiling.

This year some friends sent me a Christmas card of themselves surrounded by their children. They all look happy, they're all laughing. It's a picture that would be very difficult for us to create. For a start, you would have to make

Thomas and Mathieu laugh on command. As for us, the parents, we don't always feel like laughing.

And I can't quite picture the words "and a happy New Year" in fancy gold script just above my two kids' lumpy, shaggy-haired heads. It's more likely to look like one of Reiser's risqué covers for *Hara-Kiri* magazine than a Christmas card.

One day, seeing Josée trying to unblock a sink with a plunger, I told her I would buy another one.

"Why two?" she asked. "One's enough."

"You're forgetting I have two children," I replied.

She didn't understand so I explained that, when we took Mathieu and Thomas for a walk and had to get them over a stream, it would be practical to use plungers. You could attach them to the children's heads. Then you could just grab the handles to lift them up and get them over the stream without getting their feet wet. It was easier than carrying them in your arms.

She was horrified.

The plunger disappeared after that. She must have hidden it . . .

Mathieu and Thomas are asleep and I'm watching them.

What are they dreaming about?

Do they have dreams like other people?

Maybe at night they dream they're intelligent.

Maybe at night they have their revenge and dream the dreams of gifted children.

Maybe at night they're top engineers, scientific researchers . . . who find whatever they're looking for.

Maybe at night they discover laws and principles, postulations and theories.

Maybe at night they do endless arcane calculations.

Maybe at night they speak Latin and Greek.

But the minute the sun rises—so that no one ever guesses—they revert to looking like handicapped children. In order to be left in peace they pretend they can't talk. When someone speaks to them they act as if they don't understand. They don't want to go to school and do homework and learn lessons.

You've got to understand them, they have to be serious all night so they need to relax during the day. So they just muck about.

The only thing we got right was your names. By choosing Mathieu and Thomas we were going the safe route, with a nod toward the saints. Because you never know, and it's always best to keep on the right side of everyone.

If we were hoping to attract God's blessing on you, we kind of messed up.

To think of your feeble little limbs, you just weren't built to be called Tarzan . . . I can't really see you in the jungle, swinging from branch to branch, challenging bloodthirsty beasts, and dislocating a lion's jaw or breaking a buffalo's neck with your bare hands.

You were more like Tarzoon, the shame of the jungle.

Mind you, I prefer you to Tarzan and his arrogance. You're so much more touching, my two little birds. You remind me of E.T.

Thomas wears glasses, little red glasses, they really suit him. Along with his dungarees, they make him look like an American student—a charmer!

I can't remember how we found out he couldn't see clearly. Now that he has his glasses, everything he sees must be in sharp focus, Snoopy, his drawings . . . For a while I had the extraordinarily naive belief that he would finally be able to read. First I would buy him strip cartoons, then children's "early reader" books, then the classics: Alexandre Dumas, Jules Verne, *Le Grand Meaulnes* . . . and why not a bit of Proust.

No, he'll never be able to read. Even if the letters on the page are now clear, it will still all be a haze inside his head. He'll never know that all those tiny lines and twirls covering the pages of books tell us stories and can transport us somewhere else. Confronted with them, he's like me trying to decipher hieroglyphics.

He must think they're drawings, minute drawings that don't mean anything. Or perhaps he thinks they're lines of ants, and watches them, amazed that they don't run away when he brings his hand down to crush them.

To elicit sympathy from passersby, beggars display their misfortune, their clubfeet or amputations, their old dogs and flea-bitten cats, their children. I could do the same. I've got two good claims on people's heartstrings, all I'd have to do is put my two boys in their threadbare navy blue coats. I could sit down on a cardboard box on the ground with them and look devastated. I could have a stereo playing rousing music and Mathieu could beat in time to it on his ball.

Look, I've always wanted to be a comedian, so I could recite Vigny's stirring poem "Death of a Wolf" while Thomas did his star turn as a crying wolf, "Whooo, cries da wolf" . . .

People might be really moved and struck by the performance. They'd give us money to go and drink an absinthe to their old grandfather.

I've done something crazy, I've just bought myself a Bentley. An old one, a Mark VI, 22 horsepower, it goes through nine gallons of gas every hundred miles. It's navy blue and black, with a red leather interior. The dashboard is burled walnut, with loads of little round dials and faceted indicator lights like precious stones. It's like a beautiful old carriage; when it draws up to the sidewalk people expect the Queen of England to step out.

I use it to pick up Thomas and Mathieu from their special school, sitting them down on the back seat, like two princes.

I'm proud of my car; everyone gazes at it respectfully, trying to make out some famous passenger in the back.

If they could see what's in the back, they'd be disappointed. Instead of the Queen of England, there are two dribbling, misshapen little kids, and one of them—the really gifted one—keeps saying, "Where we going, Daddy? Where we going, Daddy?"

I remember once driving along and not being able to resist the temptation to talk to them like a father who's just picked his children up from high school. I invented questions about their schoolwork. "So, Mathieu, how did your homework on Montaigne go? What grade did you get for your essay? How about you, Thomas, how many mistakes were there in your Latin translation? And how's the trigonometry going?"

While I talked to them about their schoolwork, I watched their tousled little heads and blank expressions in the rear-view mirror. Maybe I was hoping they'd give me a proper answer, that we'd stop the whole joke about handicaps, it wasn't funny anymore, this game, and we were finally going to be sensible like everyone else, they were finally going to be like everyone else . . .

I waited quite a while for an answer.

Thomas said, "Where we going, Daddy?" several times, while Mathieu went "Brmm, brmm" . . .

It wasn't a game.

Every weekend, Thomas and Mathieu come home from special school covered in scrapes and scratches. They must fight like dogs. Alternatively—now that cockfighting's been banned, and to help make ends meet—I can see the teachers at their rural institution organizing child-fights.

Judging by how deep the gashes are, they clearly attach metal spurs to the children's fingers. Which isn't acceptable.

I'm going to have to write to the management and ask them to stop.

Thomas needn't be jealous of his brother any longer, he's going to have a brace too. An impressive surgical corset with chrome-plated metal and leather. His frame's collapsing, he's becoming hunchbacked like his brother. Soon they'll be like little old men who've spent their whole lives harvesting beetroot in the fields.

These braces cost a fortune, they're entirely handmade in a specialized workshop in Paris, near La Motte-Picquet, a place called Maison Leprêtre. Every year we have to take them to the workshop to be measured for new braces, because they're growing. They always meekly let the experts get on with it.

When they've got their braces on they look like Roman warriors in breastplates, or characters from a science fiction cartoon because of the gleaming chrome.

When you pick them up in your arms it feels like you're holding a robot. A metal doll.

It takes a monkey wrench to get them undressed at night. When you peel their breastplates off, you find purple welts left on their naked torsos by the metal stays, and all that's left are two shivering little plucked birds.

I've directed several television programs about handicapped children. I remember the first one: my opening sequence was stock footage of a beautiful baby competition, and the soundtrack was a song all about glorious, victorious youth.

I have an unusual attitude toward beautiful baby competitions. I really don't understand why anyone congratulates and rewards people who have beautiful children, as if they did it on purpose. Why, then, don't they punish and fine those who have handicapped children?

I can still see those arrogant, self-assured mothers, brandishing their masterpieces in front of the jury.

I wanted them to drop them.

I've just gotten back to the apartment. Josée is alone in the children's bedroom, the beds are both empty and the window is wide open. I lean out of it and look down, vaguely concerned.

We now live on the fourteenth floor.

Where are the kids? I can't hear them anywhere. Josée's thrown them out the window. She might have had a moment of madness; you read about that sort of thing in the papers sometimes.

"Josée, why've you thrown the boys out the window?"

I only asked it as a joke, to dispel the image.

She hasn't answered, she doesn't understand, she's speechless.

I carry on in the same tone of voice: "What you've done is very bad, Josée. I know they're handicapped, but that's no excuse to throw them out."

Josée's terrified, she looks at me in stunned silence, I think she's frightened of me. She goes into our bedroom, comes back with the children in her arms, and stands them in front of me.

They're fine.

Josée's quite shaken, she must be thinking, "Hardly surprising the boss's kids are crazy."

Mathieu and Thomas will never know Bach, Schubert, Brahms, Chopin . . .

They will never benefit from the blessings these composers have to offer, blessings that help you get through those gloomy mornings when you're feeling low and the heating has broken down. They will never know the goose bumps you get from listening to a Mozart adagio, the energy transmitted by Beethoven's roaring crescendos and Liszt's flourishes, the way Wagner makes you want to jump to your feet and go and invade Poland, Bach's fortifying dances and the warm tears shed for a mournful Schubert song . . .

I would have liked trying out stereo systems with them and buying one for them. Acting as their first deejay, buying them their first album . . .

I would have liked listening to music with them, discussing its strengths and weaknesses, comparing different interpretations, and deciding on the best . . .

Setting them aquiver with Benedetti, Gould, and Arrau on the piano, and Menuhin, Oïstrakh, and Milstein on the violin.

And giving them a glimpse of paradise.

It's autumn. I'm driving through the forest at Compiègne in my Bentley with Thomas and Mathieu in the back. The countryside is unspeakably beautiful. The whole forest is ablaze with color, glorious as a Watteau. I can't even say "Look how gorgeous it is!" to them, Thomas and Mathieu aren't looking at the scenery, they couldn't give a damn about it. We'll never be able to admire anything together.

They will never know Watteau, will never go to a museum. Those great joys that help human beings live . . . they'll be deprived of them too.

But they do still have French fries. They love fries, especially Thomas, who calls them "Fench fies."

When I'm alone in the car with Thomas and Mathieu I sometimes have weird ideas. I could buy a couple of bottles—one of camping gas and one of whiskey—and drain them both.

I think that if I had a serious car crash things might be better. Particularly for my wife. I'm more and more impossible to live with, and the boys are getting more and more difficult as they get older. So I accelerate and close my eyes, keeping them closed as long as I can.

I'll never forget the incredible doctor who saw us when my wife was pregnant for the third time. Abortion was discussed but he said, "I'm going to speak bluntly. You're in a hell of a situation. You already have two handicapped children. If you had one more, would things really change much? But imagine having a normal child this time. Everything would change. You wouldn't be finishing on a bad note, it could be the chance of a lifetime."

Our chance was called Marie; she was normal and very pretty. And why not, we already had two trial runs. The doctors, who knew about her predecessors, were reassured.

Two days after the birth, a pediatrician came to see our daughter. He examined her foot at length, then, out loud, said, "Looks like a club foot . . ." and a moment later added, "No, I'm wrong."

I'm sure he meant it as a joke.

My daughter grew and became our pride and joy. She's beautiful, she's intelligent. Sweet revenge on our fate, until the day—

No, that's enough messing around, she's another story.

The mother of my children, whom I pushed to the limit, eventually had enough: she left me. She went to laugh somewhere else. Serves me right. I deserved it.

I end up on my own, adrift.

I'd love to start over again, young and handsome.

I can just see my lonely hearts ad:

"40-year-old teenager, 3 kids (2 handicapped), seeks cultured, pretty, young woman with a sense of humor."

She's going to need a lot of that, specially the dark kind.

I've met a few cute but rather dumb girls. I was careful not to mention my children, otherwise they'd have run.

I remember a blonde who knew I had children but not what state they were in. I can still hear her saying, "When are you going to introduce me to your children, it's like you don't want to, are you ashamed of me?"

Some of the teachers at Mathieu and Thomas's special school are young women; there's one tall brunette in particular who's very pretty. That would obviously be ideal, she knows my kids and has the instruction manual.

In the end, it didn't work out. She must have thought, "I can deal with the handicapped during the week, it's my job, but if I have to spend every weekend with them too . . ." And maybe I wasn't her type either and she might have thought, "This guy specializes in handicapped children, he could easily give me one too, so no thanks."

And then, one day, once upon a time, there was a charming, cultured girl with a sense of humor. She took an interest in me and my two little kids. We were very lucky, she stayed. Thanks to her, Thomas learned to open and close a zipper. Not for long. The next day he couldn't remember how, he'd forgotten everything, we had to start the learning process from square one again.

With my children no one need ever worry about repeating themselves, my sons forget everything. With them, nothing's ever old hat, in a rut, or boring. Nothing goes out of fashion, everything's new.

My little birds, I'm so sad to think you'll never experience the thing that, for me, has constituted the greatest moments of my life.

Those extraordinary moments when the world is reduced to a single person, when you exist only for her and thanks to her, you tremble at the sound of her footsteps, the sound of her voice, and go weak at the knees when you see her. When you're afraid you might break her from holding her so tight, when every kiss is bliss and the world around you melts away.

You will never know that delicious shivering feeling that runs from your head down to your toes, throws you into turmoil, more of an upheaval than moving houses, an electrocution, an execution. Turns you upside down with your feet off the ground, makes you feel lost, makes you feel found, picks you up and spins you around. It shakes you up inside, makes you hot and cold all over, makes you flutter and makes you stutter, makes your hair stand on end, drives you around the bend, makes you say the dumbest things, makes you laugh but also makes you cry.

Because, alas, my little birds, you will never know how to conjugate the indicative mood of the first person of the present tense of the verb *to love*.

When someone in the street asks me to make a donation for handicapped children I say no.

I don't dare say I have two handicapped children, they would think I was joking.

With an offhand smile, I allow myself the luxury of saying, "Handicapped children? I've got the T-shirt."

I've just invented a bird. I've called it Grounded. It's a rare bird, not like others. It's afraid of heights. Which is tough luck for a bird. But it keeps its spirits up. Instead of feeling sorry for itself, it jokes about its handicap.

Every time someone asks it to fly, it always finds a funny excuse not to, and makes everyone laugh. It's got plenty of nerve, too, it makes fun of the birds that can fly, the normal birds.

It's as if Thomas and Mathieu could make fun of the normal children they see in the street.

Turning the world on its head.

It's raining and Josée has returned from her walk with the children. She's busy getting Mathieu to eat.

I can't see Thomas, and go out of the room. His snowsuit is hanging on the coatrack in the corridor, still puffed up, still in the shape of a body. I go back into the room stony-faced.

"Josée, why've you hung Thomas from a coat hook?"

She looks up blankly.

I persevere with my joke: "Just because he's disabled doesn't mean you can hang him on a coat hook?"

Josée didn't miss a beat and replied, "I'm leaving him to dry for a minute, he was soaked."

My children are very affectionate. In shops Thomas wants to kiss everyone, young, old, rich, poor, blacks, whites, indiscriminately.

People get quite embarrassed when they see a boy of twelve bearing down on them. Some back away, others let him get on with it and—as they wipe their faces with a hanky—they say, "He's so sweet!"

And it's true, they're sweet. They see no evil in anything, like the innocent. They date back to before original sin, to a time when the world was good, when nature was well-meaning, when every kind of mushroom was edible and you could stroke tigers safely.

When they're at the zoo, they want to kiss the tigers too. When they're at home they want to pull our cat's tail. Oddly, the cat doesn't scratch them; he must think, "They're handicapped, I have to be lenient, they're not all there in the head."

Would a tiger react in the same way if Thomas or Mathieu pulled its tail?

I'll give it a try, but I'll warn the tiger first.

When I go for walks with my two boys, it feels like having a puppet or a rag doll in each hand. They're light, they have fragile little bones, they've stopped growing or putting on weight, at fourteen they look more like seven, they're like little imps. They don't say what they want in French, they speak Impish, or they mew, roar, bark, twitter, cackle, whinny, squeal, or squeak. I don't always understand them.

What exactly is there inside my two imps' heads? It's not lead. Apart from the straw, there can't be very much there, at best a birdbrain, or a bit of old junk like a crystal set radio receptor that no longer works. A few badly soldered electrical wires, a transistor, a flickering little bulb that often goes out, and a few recorded words playing on a loop.

With a brain like that it's hardly surprising they're not high-performance. They'll never get into Polytechnique, a top-rated engineering school, which is a shame. I would have been so proud, given how terrible I've always been at math.

I had a huge surprise recently. I found Mathieu immersed in a book. Overcome with emotion, I went over to him.

He was holding the book upside down.

I've always loved the magazine *Hara-Kiri*. I once wanted to suggest a cover for it. My brother, who *does* study at Polytechnique, has an impressive uniform with a cocked hat; I wanted to borrow it and take a photo of Mathieu wearing it. I'd put some thought into the caption too: "This year our top student is a boy!"[2]

Sorry, Mathieu. I can't help it if I have twisted ideas. It wasn't to make fun of you, perhaps it was me I wanted to make fun of. To prove I could laugh at my own hardships.

2. The previous year, for the first time, the top student at Polytechnique was a girl, Anne Chopinet.

Mathieu is getting more and more hunched. Physical therapy, metal braces . . . nothing helps. At fifteen he has the silhouette of a little old man. When we take him out for a walk all he can see are his own feet, he can't even see the heavenly blue of the sky anymore.

At one point I thought of fitting the tips of his shoes with little mirrors, like wing-mirrors to reflect the heavens for him . . .

His scoliosis is getting worse and will soon cause respiratory problems. They'll have to try and operate on his spine.

They try, and he's perfectly upright again.

Three days later he drops down dead.

In the end the operation that was meant to help him see the heavens succeeded.

My little boy's gorgeous, he's always laughing, he's got beady little black eyes like a rat.

I'm often afraid of losing him. He's only two centimeters tall . . . even though he's ten.

When he was born we were surprised, rather worried even. The doctor set our minds at rest right away by saying, "He's completely normal, be patient, he's just a little backward, he'll grow." We're patient, we're impatient, he's not growing.

Ten years later the nick we made in the skirting board to mark his height when he was a year old is still valid.

No school has agreed to take him, on the grounds that he's not like the others. We have to keep him at home. We've had to hire a home tutor. It's very hard finding anyone who'll take the job. It involves a lot of care and responsibility; he's so small, people are afraid of losing him.

Particularly because he's such a practical joker, he loves hiding and doesn't answer when he's called. We spend so much time looking for him: we have to empty the pockets of all our clothes, search through all the drawers and open every box. Last time he hid in a matchbox.

Washing him is difficult, there's always the fear he could drown in the basin. Or get swept down the drain. The hardest thing is cutting his fingernails.

To find out his weight we have to take him to the post office and put him on the letter scales.

He had a terrible toothache recently. No dentist was prepared to treat him, I had to take him to a clockmaker.

Every time friends and relations see him they say, "Look how much he's grown." I don't believe them, I know they're only saying it to make us happy.

Once a doctor who was braver than the others told us he would never grow. It was a hard blow.

Gradually we got used to it, we could see the advantages.

We can keep him on us, lay our hands on him at any time, he's no trouble, you can just slip him in a pocket, he doesn't need a ticket on public transport, but most of all he's very affectionate, he loves checking us over for head lice.

One day we lost him.

I spent the whole night lifting up dead leaves, one by one.

It was autumn.

It was a dream.

No one should think it's less sad when a handicapped child dies. It's just as sad as when a normal child dies.

It's a terrible thing, the death of someone who's never been happy, someone who came and spent a bit of time on earth just to suffer.

With someone like that it's a struggle remembering a single smile.

They say we'll see each other again one day, the three of us.

Will we recognize each other? What will you be like? What will you be wearing? I've always seen you in dungarees, perhaps you'll be in three-piece suits, or in white robes like angels? Maybe you'll have moustaches or beards, to look grown-up? Will you have changed, will you have grown?

Will you recognize me? I'm likely to be in a terrible state when I get there.

I won't dare ask if you're still handicapped . . . Do handicaps even exist in heaven? Maybe you'll be like everyone else?

Will we be able to speak man to man, and tell each other things that really matter, things I couldn't say to you on earth because you didn't understand French and I couldn't speak Impish?

Perhaps in heaven we'll finally be able to understand each other. And, more importantly, we'll meet up with your grandfather. The person I could never tell you about and whom you never knew. You'll soon see he was an extraordinary man, I'm sure you'll like him and he'll make you laugh.

He'll take you for a spin in his sports car, he'll have you drinking, they must drink mead up there.

He'll drive so fast in his car, very fast, too fast. No one will be frightened.

There's nothing to be afraid of, you're already dead.

For a while we were worried that Thomas was upset by his brother's death. At first he looked for him everywhere, opening cupboards and drawers, but not for long. His various activities—drawing, taking care of Snoopy—took over again. Thomas loves painting and drawing. His leanings are toward abstracts. He hasn't been through a figurative period, he went straight to abstract. He's very prolific and never touches up his work afterward. He produces series, and always gives them the same title. There are the "For Daddy" pictures, the "For Mommy" pictures, and the "For my sister Marie" pictures.

His style isn't evolving much, it's still fairly close to Pollock's. His palette is bright. The format is always the same. He gets so carried away he often goes beyond the edge of the paper and continues the work on the table, directly onto the wood.

When he's finished a picture he gives it to one of us. And when we tell him it's lovely he seems happy.

I sometimes get postcards from a holiday camp the children go to. It's often an orange sunset over the sea or a glittering mountain. On the back it says, "Dear Daddy, I'm very happy and having lots of fun. I'm thinking of you." It's signed Thomas.

The writing is tidy and regular, there are no spelling mistakes, the instructor has taken her time. She thought it would make me happy. I understand her good intentions.

It doesn't make me happy.

I prefer Thomas's shapeless, illegible scribblings. Maybe with those abstract drawings of his he's actually saying more to me.

Pierre Desproges[3] came with me once to pick Thomas up from his school. He didn't really want to but I insisted.

Like any newcomer, he was descended upon by lurching, dribbling—and not always very alluring—children wanting to kiss him. For someone who has trouble tolerating his own peers and is often quite reserved when confronted with his groupies' exuberant enthusiasm, he succumbed to their attentions with good grace.

He was very moved by that visit. He wanted to go back. He was fascinated by that strange world where twenty-year-old children smother their teddy bears with kisses, come and take you by the hand, or threaten to cut you in two with a pair of scissors.

He'd always loved the absurd; now he'd found some masters of the art.

3. Pierre Desproges (1939–1988), outspoken and eloquent French humorist.

When I think of Mathieu and Thomas, I see them as two tousled little birds. Not eagles or peacocks, but modest birds, sparrows.

Their spindly little legs sticking out from under their short navy blue coats. I also remember, from bath time, their mauve transparent skin, like baby birds before they grow feathers; I remember their prominent breastbones and their ribs sticking out along their torsos. Their brains were birdlike too.

All that was missing were the wings.

Shame.

They could have gotten away from this world that wasn't right for them.

They'd have gotten out more quickly, on the wing.

I've never talked about my two boys until now. Why not? Was I ashamed? Afraid of being pitied?

A combination of both. I think it was mainly to avoid the terrible question: "What do they do?"

I could have invented things . . .

"Thomas is in the States, at the Massachusetts Institute of Technology. He's studying for a degree in particle accelerators. He's happy, it's going well, he's met a young American girl called Marilyn, such a beautiful girl, I'm sure he's going to settle over there."

"Isn't that a bit hard for you, him being so far away?"

"America's not the end of the earth. And what really matters is that he's happy. We get all his news, he calls his mother once a week. But Mathieu, who's interning with an architect in Sydney, never gets in touch anymore . . ."

I could have told the truth too.

"Do you really want to know what they do? Mathieu doesn't do anything anymore, he's no longer with us. Didn't you know? No, don't apologize, the death of a handicapped child often goes unnoticed. People talk in terms of release . . .

"Thomas is still here, lurking in the corridors of his special school, clutching a chewed old doll and talking to his hand with weird screaming noises."

"But he must be quite big now, how old is he?"

"No, he's not big. Old, yes, but not big. He'll never be big. You never get big when your head's full of straw."

When I was little I used to do the most outlandish things to attract attention. Aged six, I would steal a herring from the fishmonger on market day, and my great game was to chase girls and rub my fish over their bare legs.

In high school, wanting to appear romantic and like Byron, I wore floppy cravats instead of ties, and, wanting to be an iconoclast, I put the statue of the Virgin Mary in the restrooms.

Every time I went into a shop to try something on I only had to hear the words "They've been very popular, I must have sold ten of them yesterday" to decide against buying the thing. I didn't want to be like everyone else.

Later, when I started working in television and was entrusted with small directing projects, I always tried—with varying degrees of success—to find an unusual camera angle.

I remember an anecdote about the painter Édouard Pignon, who was the subject of a television documentary I made. When he was painting the trunks of some olive trees a child walked past; after looking at the painting, the child said, "It doesn't look like anything, what you're doing there." Flattered, Pignon replied, "You've just given me the most wonderful compliment, there's nothing harder than doing something that doesn't look like any-thing else."

My boys don't look like anyone else. To think I always wanted to do things differently—I should be glad.

At any given time, in every school, in every town, somewhere at the back of the class, usually near the radiator, there will always be a child with a vacant expression. Every time he gets up or opens his mouth to answer a question, the others know they're going to laugh. His answers are always completely random, because he hasn't understood the question, he never will. Sometimes the teacher is sadistic and probes the child further, playing to the gallery, livening things up and raising his own ratings.

The child with the vacant expression, standing there in the middle of his giggling and whooping classmates, doesn't want to make anyone laugh, he doesn't do it on purpose, quite the opposite. He'd like not to make people laugh, he'd like to understand, he tries hard to, but despite his efforts he says stupid things, because it's not within his scope to get the point.

When I was a kid I was the first to laugh; now I feel tremendous compassion for that child with the vacant expression. I think of my own two boys.

Luckily, no one will actually be able to make fun of them at school. They'll never go to school.

I've never liked the word "handicapped." It's got depressing overtones of the expression "cap in hand."

I don't like the word "abnormal" either, especially when it's hooked up with "child."

What does "normal" mean? How we should be, how we ought to be, in other words average, standard-issue. I don't really like average things, I prefer things that aren't average, things that are above average and–why not?– below; different, anyway. I prefer the expression "not like other people." Because other people aren't always that great if you ask me.

Not being like other people doesn't necessarily mean you're not as good as them, it just means being different from them.

What would it mean if a bird wasn't like other birds? It could just as easily mean a bird with a fear of heights as one that could sing all of Mozart's flute sonatas without the score.

A cow that's not like other cows might know how to make phone calls.

When I talk about my children I say they're "not like other people." It leaves a glimmer of doubt.

Einstein, Mozart, Michelangelo . . . they weren't like other people.

If you'd been like other people, I would have taken you to museums. We could have looked at great paintings together, Rembrandts, Monets, Turners, and more Rembrandts . . .

If you'd been like other people, I would have given you recordings of classical music and we could have listened to them together, first Mozart, then Beethoven, Bach, and Mozart again.

If you'd been like other people, I would have given you loads of books by Prévert, Marcel Aymé, Queneau, Ionesco, and more Prévert.

If you'd been like other people, I would have taken you to the movies, we could have watched all those old films together, Chaplin, Eisenstein, Hitchcock, Buñuel, and more Chaplin.

If you'd been like other people, I would have taken you to smart restaurants, I would have given you Chambolle-Musigny to drink and then some more Chambolle-Musigny.

If you'd been like other people, we would have played tennis together, and basketball and volleyball.

If you'd been like other people, we would have climbed the bell towers of Gothic cathedrals together to have a bird's-eye view.

If you'd been like other people, I would have bought you the latest clothes, so you could be the best looking.

If you'd been like other people, I would have driven you to parties with your girlfriends in my old convertible.

If you'd been like other people, we would have had a huge reception for your weddings.

If you'd been like other people, I would have had grand-children.

If you'd been like other people, I might not have been so afraid of the future.

But if you'd been like other people, you would have been like everyone else.

Maybe you wouldn't have achieved anything in school.

You'd have been a couple of delinquents.

You'd have taken the mufflers off your scooters to make more noise.

You'd have been unemployed.

You'd have liked Jean-Michel Jarre.

You'd have married dumb broads.

You'd have gotten divorced.

And maybe you'd have had handicapped children.

What a narrow escape!

I've had my cat castrated, without warning him and without asking his permission. Without explaining the advantages and drawbacks to him. I just told him he was having his tonsils out. I get the feeling he's been sulking at me ever since. I don't dare look him in the eye now. I feel remorseful.

I think back to the days when they wanted to sterilize handicapped children. Well, polite society can relax, my children won't reproduce. I won't have grandchildren, I won't go for walks with a little hand bobbing up and down in my old bony hand. No one will ask me where the sun goes when it sets, no one will call me Grandpa, except for young assholes in the car behind telling me I'm not driving fast enough. The lineage will come to an end, we'll stop there. And it's better that way.

Parents should only have normal children; they could all win equal first place at the beautiful baby competition and, later, in their school exams. Abnormal children should be banned.

It's not really a problem for my little birds, no one need worry. They'll never cause much trouble with their tiny little willies.

I've just bought a secondhand American car, a Camaro. It's dark green with a white leatherette interior, a bit flashy.

We're going to Portugal for a holiday.

We're taking Thomas with us, he's going to see the sea. We've picked him up from La Source, the special school he attends near Tours.

The Camaro glides along the road, silently.

After spending a night in Spain, we arrive in Sagres, our destination. The hotel is white, the sky blue, and the light over the sea intense, almost African.

How wonderful to be here at last. We get Thomas out and he's thrilled; he looks at the hotel and claps his hands and cries, "La Source, La Source!" He thinks he's back at his school. Perhaps he's dazzled by the sun, or it's a joke, he's saying it to make us laugh.

The hotel is a bit precious, the staff are dressed in wine-colored uniforms with gold buttons. The waiters all wear badges with their names on them, ours is called Victor Hugo. Thomas wants to kiss everyone.

Thomas is served at the table like a little prince. What he doesn't like is the way the maître d' removes the presentation plates from the table before serving us. He gets angry, hangs onto his plate, won't let anyone take it from him and cries, "No, mister man! Not my plate, not my plate!" He must think that if someone takes his plate he won't get anything to eat.

Thomas is frightened of the ocean, the noise of its great waves. I try to get him used to it. I walk into the water with him in my arms, he clings to me, terrified. I'll never forget the terror in his eyes. One day he finds a trick to stop this torture and make us take him out of the water: he adopts a tragic expression and—shouting really loudly so we can hear him over the crashing waves—says "Poop!" Thinking it's urgent, I take him out of the water.

I soon realize it isn't true. I'm overcome. Thomas is no fool, there are a few sparks in his little birdbrain.

He is capable of lying.

Mathieu and Thomas will never have subway cards or pre-paid parking cards in their wallets. They'll never have wallets and their only card will be a disability card.

It's the color orange, to be cheerful. It has the words "marked musculoskeletal impairment" in green letters.

It was supplied by the local authorities in Paris.

Their degree of disability, in percentage terms, is 80 percent.

The local authority has no illusions about their development, it has supplied the cards for an "indefinite" period.

The cards have their pictures on them. Their funny faces, their vacant expressions . . . What are they thinking about?

I still use them now. I sometimes put them on my windshield when I've parked illegally. Thanks to them I can avoid a fine.

My children will never have a résumé. What have they done? Nothing. Kind of convenient, no one will ever ask anything of them.

What could you put on their résumés? Abnormal childhood, admitted long-term to special school, first La Source, then Le Cèdre–The Source and The Cedar Tree, they get all the best names!

My children will never have a criminal record. They're innocent. They haven't done anything wrong, they wouldn't know how to.

Sometimes, in winter, when I see them in balaclavas, I picture them as bank robbers. They wouldn't be very dangerous with their unconvincing gestures and shaky hands.

The police would catch them easily, they wouldn't run away, they can't run.

I'll never understand why they've been so heavily punished. It's profoundly unfair, they haven't done anything wrong.

It's like a terrible miscarriage of justice.

In an unforgettable sketch, Pierre Desproges takes revenge on his young children and the horrors they give him on Father's Day.

I haven't actually needed revenge. I've never been given anything. No presents, no loving notes, nothing.

On that particular day, though, I'd have paid through the nose for a yogurt pot transformed into a receptacle for loose change by Mathieu. He would have wrapped it in mauve felt and decorated it by sticking on stars he had cut from gold paper all by himself.

On that particular day I'd have paid through the nose for a badly written note from Thomas in which he'd toiled to form the words "i luv yoo verry mutch."

On that particular day I'd have paid through the nose for an ashtray as gnarled as a Jerusalem artichoke that Mathieu had made out of modeling clay and engraved with the word *Daddy*.

Because they're not like other people, they could have given me presents unlike other presents. On that particular day I'd have paid through the nose for a pebble, a dried leaf, a bluebottle, a horse chestnut, a ladybug . . .

Because they're not like other people, they could have done drawings for me unlike other drawings. On that particular day I'd have paid through the nose for odd-shaped animals like weird Dubuffet-style camels and Picasso-style horses.

They didn't do anything.

Not because they were unwilling, not because they didn't want to, I think they would have wanted to, but they couldn't. Because of their shaky hands, their poorly focused eyes, and the straw inside their heads.

Dear Daddy,

Because it's Father's Day, we wanted to write you a letter. So here it is.

We won't congratulate you on what you've produced: take a look at us. Was it that hard making children like everyone else? When you know how many normal children are born every day and you see what some parents look like, you've got to think it's not rocket science.

We weren't asking you to produce mini geniuses, just normal kids. Once again you wanted to be different. Well, you won, and we lost out. Do you think it's fun being hand-icapped? We do have a few advantages. We've avoided going to school, no homework, no lessons, no exams, no punishments. On the other hand, no rewards, we missed out on quite a lot of stuff.

Maybe Mathieu would have liked playing soccer. Can you see him out on the field, a fragile little thing amidst great strong brutes? He wouldn't have come out alive.

Do you think it's fun spending your life with handicapped people? Some of them are really difficult, they scream the whole time and stop us from getting to sleep, and there are vicious ones who bite.

Because we don't bear grudges and we're fond of you, we're going to wish you a happy Father's Day.

On the back of this letter there's a picture I've done for you. Mathieu can't draw so he just sends you a kiss.

Children who are not like the others aren't some sort of nationwide specialty, there are several different versions.

In the special school that Thomas and Mathieu go to there's a Cambodian child. His parents don't speak very good French, their meetings with the head doctor of the establishment are difficult, sometimes epic. They often come out very upset. They always strenuously challenge the doctor's diagnosis.

Their son isn't a Mongoloid, he's Cambodian.

Nobody mention genetics, it's bad luck.

I'm not the one who thought of genetics, it's genetics that thought of me.

I look at my two misshapen little kids and hope it's not my fault they're not like other people.

But the fact that they can't speak, they can't write, they can't count to a hundred, they can't ride a bike, they can't swim, they can't play the piano, they can't tie their shoelaces, they can't eat mussels, they can't use computers . . . surely that isn't because I haven't brought them up properly, it's not because of their environment . . .

Look at them. It's not my fault if they're lame and hunchbacked. It's the fault of just being unlucky.

Maybe "genetics" is the technical term for being unlucky?

My daughter Marie told her school friends she had two handicapped brothers. They wouldn't believe her. They said it wasn't true, she was showing off.

There are some mothers who stand over their children's cots and say, "I don't want him to grow up, I wish he could stay like this forever." The mothers of handicapped children are very lucky, they can play dolls for longer.

But one day the doll will weigh seventy pounds and it won't always be docile.

Fathers take an interest in their children when they're older, when they're inquisitive and start asking questions.

I waited in vain for that time. There was only ever one question: "Where we going, Daddy?"

The best gift you can give any child is to provide answers to their curiosity, give them a taste for the wonderful things in life. I never had the opportunity with Mathieu and Thomas.

I'd have really liked being a teacher, helping children learn things without boring them.

I've made cartoons for children that my own kids haven't seen, and written books they haven't read.

I would have liked them to be proud of me. For them to say "My dad's better than yours" to their friends.

If children need to feel proud of their fathers, then perhaps, as a form of reassurance, fathers need their children's admiration.

In the days when there used to be a test card between television programs, Mathieu and Thomas were quite capable of sitting and watching it for hours. Thomas likes television, particularly since the day he saw me on it. He doesn't even have good eyesight but he managed to make me out in the middle of a group of people on a small screen. He recognized me and cried out, "Daddy!"

After the program he wouldn't come and eat, he wanted to stay in front of the TV. He kept shouting, "Daddy, Daddy!" He thought I would come back.

Perhaps I'm wrong when I think I don't mean much to him and he could easily live without me. I find it touching but it makes me feel guilty too. I can't really see myself living with him, going to the supermarket every day to look at the Snoopies.

Thomas will be fourteen soon. At his age I was taking my first major exams.

I'm looking at Thomas. I really struggle to see myself in him, we're not alike. Maybe it's better that way. I can't say for which of us. Whatever made me want to reproduce myself?

Pride? Was I so pleased with myself I wanted to leave little copies of myself on the planet?

Did I want to leave some trace, so that someone could follow me?

Sometimes I feel I *have* left a trace, but the sort you leave when you've walked over a waxed wooden floor with muddy shoes and someone yells at you.

When I look at Thomas, and when I think of Mathieu, I wonder whether I did the right thing making them.

Have to ask them.

At the end of the day, if you put all their little pleasures end to end—Snoopy, a warm bath, a cat rubbing against them, a ray of sun, a ball, a walk to the supermarket, a stranger's smile, toy cars, French fries—I hope it makes their time here bearable.

Something has just reminded me of a white dove at the children's special school, in the workshop where they did art, daubing paint over sheets of paper.

When the white dove flies across the room some of the children clap their hands in wonderment. From time to time it drops a little feather that zigzags its way to the floor, watched by at least one pair of eyes. There's a sort of peacefulness in the workshop, perhaps because of the dove. Occasionally it comes to land on a table or, better still, on a child's shoulder. You can't help thinking of Picasso, of *Child with a Dove*. Some of them are afraid and scream in terror. But it's a good-natured dove. Thomas runs after it calling it "li'l chicken." He wants to catch it, perhaps to pluck it?

The world of man and beasts has rarely seen such harmony. Something is communicated between the two bird-brains. Saint Francis of Assisi isn't far away, neither is Giotto with his paintings full of birds.

The innocent have their hands full. Full of paint.

Thomas is eighteen, he's grown, he has trouble standing upright, the brace isn't enough, he needs a stake, a support. I've been chosen.

A stake has to have its feet deeply embedded in the earth, it has to be strong and stable, able to stand up to the wind, it has to stay upright in a storm.

Funny idea to have chosen me.

I now oversee his money, I have to sign his checks. Thomas couldn't give a damn about money, he doesn't really know what it is. I remember one day in a restaurant in Portugal he took all the bills from my wallet and handed them out to everyone. I'm sure that if I asked Thomas his opinion, if he had one to give, he would say, "Go on, Dad, make the most of it, let's have some fun, let's blow my disability allowances together."

He's no skinflint. We could buy ourselves a beautiful convertible with his money. We could set off like two old friends wanting to party, looking for a good time. We'd go down to the coast, like they do in films, we'd go to fancy hotels full of candelabras, and eat in big restaurants, we'd drink champagne and talk about cars, books, music, movies, girls . . .

We'd walk along the seafront in the dark, strolling over huge deserted beaches. We'd watch phosphorescent fish leave luminous trails in the black water. We'd philosophize about life, death, and God. We'd look at the stars and the lights glimmering along the coast. We'd have rows, because we wouldn't have the same opinions about everything. He'd call me a stupid old asshole and I'd say, "Have some respect, please, I'm your father," and he'd say, "That's nothing to be proud of."

A handicapped child has the right to vote.

Thomas has come of age, he's going to be able to vote. I'm sure he's thought long and hard about it, weighed the pros and cons, meticulously analyzed both candidates' policies and economic viability, he's inventoried the administrative staff of both parties.

He's still hesitating, he can't make up his mind.

Snoopy or Garfield.

After a silence he suddenly said, "How are your boys?"

He obviously didn't even know one of them has been gone for several years.

There was probably a lull in the conversation, he didn't want the social death of an awkward pause. The meal was over, everyone had talked about their news, the mood needed rekindling. The master of the house had the knowing twinkle of someone with a good joke to tell as he added, "Did you know Jean-Louis has two handicapped children?"

The information was greeted with deafening silence, then a strange murmuring, a combination of compassion, amazement, and curiosity from those who didn't know. One charming woman started gazing at me with the sad moist-eyed smile women have in paintings by Greuze.

Yes, my news is my handicapped children, but I don't always feel like talking about them.

What the master of the house expected of me was to make people laugh. A perilous undertaking but I did my best.

I told them about the previous Christmas at the institute the boys went to. How the children knocked over the Christmas tree, the choir in which everyone was singing a different tune, the Christmas tree then catching fire, the movie projector falling over during a screening, the cream cake being turned upside down, and the parents on all fours under the tables avoiding blows from some *pétanque* balls that one ill-advised father had just given to his son who was now tossing them up in the air, and all of this with "Away in a Manger" playing in the background.

At first they were slightly embarrassed, they didn't dare laugh. Then, gradually, they dared to. I was a triumph. The master of the house was pleased.

I think I'll be asked again.

Thomas talks to his hand, he calls it Martine. He has long conversations with Martine, she must talk back but he's the only one who hears her.

He puts on a soft little voice to say nice things to her. Sometimes he raises his voice at her, apparently not at all happy; Martine must have said something he doesn't like, so he shouts and yells at her.

Maybe he's annoyed with her for not being good at things?

It has to be said Martine isn't very adept and doesn't help him much in his everyday life, with getting dressed and eating. She's not accurate, she knocks his glass over when he's drinking, she fumbles, she can't button up shirts or tie shoelaces, she often gets the shakes . . .

She doesn't even know how to stroke the cat properly, her stroking is more like hitting, and the cat gets frightened and runs away.

She can't play the piano, she can't drive a car, she can't even write, she's only just up to doing abstract paintings. Maybe Martine answers back, saying it's not her fault, she's waiting for orders. It's not her job to take the initiative, it's his.

She's just a hand.

"Hello, Thomas, it's Daddy on the phone."

Total silence.

I can hear very loud, labored breathing and the teacher's voice:

"Can you hear, Thomas? It's Daddy."

"Hello, Thomas, do you know it's me? It's Daddy. How are you, Thomas?"

Silence. Just the labored breathing . . . Eventually Thomas starts talking. Since his voice broke it's powerful and loud.

"Where we going, Daddy?"

He's recognized me. We can get on with the conversation.

"How are you, Thomas?"

"Where we going, Daddy?"

"Have you done some nice pictures for Daddy and Mommy and your sister Marie?"

Silence. Just the labored breathing.

"Are we going home?"

"Have you done some nice pictures?"

"Martine."

"How's Martine?"

"Fench fies Fench fies Fench fies!"

"Did you have French fries? Were they good? . . . Do you want some French fries?"

Silence . . .

"Can you give Daddy a kiss? Can you say good-bye to Daddy? Can you give me a kiss?"

Silence.

I can hear the receiver dangling on its own, voices in the background. The teacher's on the phone again, telling me Thomas has dropped the receiver, he's gone.

I hang up.

We'd said all the important stuff.

Thomas isn't very well. He's jumpy in spite of the tranquilizers. He sometimes has outbursts where he's very violent. Every now and then he has to be confined to a psychiatric hospital . . .

We're going to see him next week, for lunch. It's nearly Christmas so I told his instructor I would bring him a present, but asked her what I should get.

She told me they listen to music all day long. All sorts of music, even classical. One of the residents whose parents are musicians listens to Mozart and Berlioz. I thought of the *Goldberg Variations*, a score J. S. Bach wrote to soothe the neurotic Count Keyserling. There were bound to be plenty of Count Keyserlings needing soothing at the institute, J. S. Bach could only help.

I've bought the album for them. The instructor's going to try the experiment.

If Bach could replace Prozac one day . . .

Thirty years later I've come across the birth announcements for Thomas and Mathieu in the bottom of a drawer. They were classic announcements; we liked things simple, no flowers or storks.

The paper has yellowed, but I have no trouble reading the beautiful typeface saying we were very happy to announce the birth of Mathieu and, later, Thomas.

Of course we were happy, it was a rare moment, a unique experience, an intense emotion, a joy you couldn't put into words . . .

The disappointment measured up to it.

We are sad to inform you that Mathieu and Thomas are handicapped, their heads are full of straw, they'll never study anything, they'll get things wrong all their lives, Mathieu will be very unhappy and will soon leave us. Thomas, though fragile, will stay longer, growing more hunched by the day . . . He talks to his hand the whole time, has difficulty walking, has stopped drawing, isn't as cheerful as he used to be, he's stopped asking where we going, Daddy.

Maybe he's happy where he is.

Or perhaps he no longer feels like going anywhere . . .

When I receive birth announcements I never feel like replying or congratulating the happy winners.

Of course I'm jealous. But later I'm mainly irritated, when the parents with their beatific smiles and smug admiration show me photos of their adorable child. They quote his latest amusing remarks and talk about how well he's doing. I find them arrogant and vulgar. Like someone boasting about how his Porsche performs to the owner of a 2CV.

"He's only four and he can already read and count . . ."

I'm not spared anything, they show me birthday photographs of the little darling blowing out his four candles—having counted them—with the father filming it all in the background. I have horrible thoughts then, I picture the candles setting fire to the tablecloth, the curtains, the whole house.

I'm sure your children are the most beautiful in the world and the most intelligent. And mine the ugliest and the stupidest. It's my fault, I got them wrong.

At fifteen Thomas and Mathieu couldn't read or write, and could barely talk.

It's a long time since I've been to see Thomas. I went to see him yesterday. He spends more and more time in a wheelchair now. He finds it difficult getting around. After a while he recognized me and asked, "Where we going, Daddy?"

He's increasingly hunched. He wanted to go for a walk outside. Our conversations are cursory and repetitive. He speaks less than he used to, but still talks to his hand.

He took us to his bedroom. It's light and painted yellow, with Snoopy still on the bed. On the wall is an abstract painting from his early days, a sort of spider caught up in its web.

He's moved to a different building, a small unit of a dozen residents, adults who look more like overaged children. They're ageless, unchanging. They must have been born on a sort of February 30th . . .

The oldest of them smokes a pipe and sticks his tongue out at the caregivers. One of them is blind and wanders down corridors feeling his way along the walls. Some say hello to us, most ignore us. Occasionally you hear a cry, then silence, just the sound of the blind man's slippers.

You have to step over a few residents lying on the floor in the middle of the room, gazing at the ceiling; they're dreaming, sometimes they laugh ecstatically.

It's not a sad place; it's strange, sometimes beautiful. Some of them waft their limbs slowly through the air creating a sort of choreography, movements from modern dance or Kabuki theater. One twists and spins his arms around in front of his face, reminding me of Egon Schiele's self-portraits.

At one of the tables there are a couple of partially sighted people sitting stroking each other's hands. At another sits a resident who is almost bald with a few wisps of gray hair; it's easy imagining him in a gray suit, he looks like an accountant, except he's wearing a bib and keeps saying, "Poop, poop, poop . . ."

Everything is allowed, every eccentricity, every whim, no one is judged.

If you're sensible and behave normally you feel almost embarrassed, you get the feeling you're not like the others and, therefore, slightly ridiculous.

When I go there I feel like being silly just like the rest of them.

At the institute everything's difficult, or even impossible. Getting dressed, tying shoelaces, doing up a belt, opening a zipper, holding a fork.

I watch an old child of twenty as his caregiver tries to get him to eat peas on his own. I suddenly grasp the accomplishment required to carry out the tiniest tasks in everyday life.

Occasionally there are minor victories worthy of Olympic gold medals. He has just scooped several peas onto the fork, and brought them up to his mouth without dropping them all. He's very proud and looks up at us, beaming. I could happily play the national anthem to honor him and his coach.

The following week there is a big sporting competition at the institute, the thirteenth Interschools games, intended for the least handicapped residents. There are several disciplines: bowling, tricycle circuits, basketball, accurate throwing, motorized circuits, and target shooting. I can't help thinking of Reiser's drawing of the Paralympics. The stadium bristles with large banners with the words "No laughing" on them.

Obviously Thomas is not taking part. He'll be a spectator. They'll take him outside and position his wheelchair by the sports ground to watch the proceedings. I'd be surprised if he was interested, he's more and more locked away in his own world. What does he think about?

Does he know what he meant to me, more than thirty years ago, the luminous little blond cherub who laughed all the time? Now he looks like a gargoyle, he dribbles and doesn't laugh anymore.

At the end of the competition they announce the results and hand out medals and cups.

I'd have loved to have children I could be proud of. To be able to show my friends your diplomas and prizes and all the cups you would have won for sports. We would have displayed them in a cabinet in the living room with pictures of us together.

In the pictures I would have the smug, satisfied smile of an angler photographed with the huge fish he's just caught.

When I was young I wanted to have swarms of children when I grew up. I could see myself climbing mountains and singing, crossing oceans with mini sailors who looked like me, traveling the world at the head of a jubilant gaggle of bright-eyed inquisitive children whom I could teach all sorts of things, the names of trees and birds and stars.

Children I could teach to play basketball and volleyball, I could have matches with and not always win.

Children I could show pictures to and play music for.

Children I could secretly teach to swear.

Children I could edify with every possible rendition of the word *fart*.

Children I could tell how a combustion engine works.

Children I could invent funny stories for.

I didn't get lucky. I played genetic lottery, and lost.

"How old are your children now?"

What the hell do you care.

My children can't be dated. Mathieu is beyond all that and Thomas must be around a hundred years old.

They're two stooped little old men. They're not all there in the head but they're still kind and affectionate.

My children have never known how old they were. Thomas still chews an ancient teddy bear, he doesn't know he's old, no one's told him.

When they were little we had to change their shoes and buy the next size up every year. Only their feet grew, their IQs didn't follow suit. Over the years they seem to have gone down instead. They've made progress in reverse.

When you've had children who play with building blocks and have teddy bears their whole life, you stay young. You don't really know where you stand anymore.

I'm not sure who I am now, I'm not sure where I've gotten to, I don't know how old I am. I still think I'm thirty years old and don't care about anything. I feel as if I've been launched into some huge practical joke, I'm not sensible, I don't take anything seriously. Here I am still talking nonsense, and writing it. My road comes to a dead end, my life ends in deadlock.

NOTE ON THE AUTHOR

Jean-Louis Fournier is a writer, humorist, and television
producer. He is the author of a number of successful
essays and novels in which the humor and humanity of
his style always shine, among others *Il a jamais tué personne
mon papa* (*My Daddy Never Killed Anyone*) (Stock, 1999)
and *Mon dernier cheveu noir* (*My Last Black Hair*) (Éditions
Anne Carrière, 2006).

NOTE ON THE CONTRIBUTORS

ADRIANA HUNTER studied French & Drama at the University of London. She has translated nearly forty books including works by Agnès Desarthe, Amélie Nothomb, Frédéric Beigbeder, Véronique Ovaldé, and Catherine Millet, and has been short-listed for the Independent Foreign Fiction Prize twice. She lives in Norfolk, England, with her husband and their three children.

FERN KUPFER is a novelist who has written for popular magazines including *Redbook, Family Circle,* and *Women's Day.* For more than a decade she wrote a column for the Long Island newspaper *Newsday*, and is the author of *Before and After Zachariah*, a memoir about family life with a severely disabled child. She is currently an associate professor of English at Iowa State University in Ames, Iowa, where she lives with her husband, writer Joseph Geha.